OM

THE TIMELESS SOUND

NASIR ZAIDI

ISBN 979-888546734-6

This book is dedicated to my friend Vijay.

This dedication is also shared with Aai & Appa

&

Professor V. Rajaraman, who always believed in me.

Contents

Contents

Acknowledgements

I believe without parents' blessings nothing is possible. So, a garland of gratitude for my father and mother.

A bouquet of thanks to my wife Farhat for patiently listening me read out the poems to her.

A rose of appreciation each for my son Saamish & my daughter Insia for lighting up my life.

A garden of gratefulness to my sisters (late) Yasmeen & Zarin & to my brother Afsar & their families for their support and motivation.

My thanks are to my Rose Manor Garden School (RMGS) mates for constantly encouraging me. We have a WhatsApp school group on which I post my writings regularly. Every post of mine is well-received by them. Special thanks are to Varsha for the cover design, to Amee for the blurb, to Dipan for the foreword, to Leena for agreeing to read the MS & to Atul, Nilesh & Nikunj for lively discussions on Om & related topics.

I would also like to put on record that while writing Om: The Timeless Sound, the Bhagavad – Gita was my constant companion. During this time, I also read Radhanath Swami Maharaj's article called Krishna is the Absolute Truth published in The Indian Express (21 April 2018) & blogs of Murari Das and soul-stirring quotes of Amit Ray. Thank you to all of them for increasing my knowledge about Om.

Thanks to everyone on the Notion team who helped in making the book attractive and pleasing to look at. Special thanks to Niveditha Hariharan, the ever-supportive, the ever-patient Publishing Manager.

Foreword

As a child I learned that Om has over a hundred meanings; one of them is 'welcome to the Gods'. Over that last four decades this has stayed with me. But this also intrigued me; I had more questions on my mind: about the other meanings; the origin of the word; other uses, etc.

Over the years, I studied, learned practiced and discovered more about Om.

Om is not about a religion, or about any practices. Om is about our existence, the first sound and is also all encompassing in that, it stands for the "whole of the Vedas". The sound of Om is the foundation, has existed since the beginning of time and mentioned in ancient Sanskrit texts. Modern religions are based on these ancient texts.

All existence around us is energy or, vibration. It is there whether we tune in or not. Thus, the whole existence is a kind of sound. If you become silent and the mind becomes subtle, you hear the sound. You hear the basic, the primordial sound "Om" as a continuous hum. The foundation or the basis of all vibration, thus all energy and hence all existence is "Om". Om is omnipresent.

It is mentioned in the Mandukya Upanishad:

Hari Om. Om-ity-etad-aksharam-idam sarvam,
tasyopavyakhyanam bhutam bhavad bhavishyaditi sarvam-omkara
eva. Yaccanyat trikalatitam tadapy omkara eva.

"All is OM: Hari Om. The whole universe is the syllable Om. Everything that was, is, or will be is, in truth Om. All else which transcends time, space, and causation is also Om."

The Kathopanisad states:

sarve veda yatpadamamananti tapamsi sarvani ca yadvadanti
yadicchanto brahmacaryam caranti tatte padmsamgrahena
bravimyomityetat.

"The goal which all the Vedas uniformly extol, which all acts of *tapas* speak of, and wishing for which men lead the life of a Brahmacharin, that goal I tell you briefly—It is this—Om."

Om is thus the Absolute Truth manifest in sound.

Every Vedic mantra is preceded by Om. Sri Krsna says in Bhagavad Gita that He is the syllable "Om" in the Vedic mantras (BG 7.8). And hence, chanting "Om" is directly chanting Krishna's name.

raso 'ham apsu kaunteya prabhasmi shashi-suryayoh
pranavah sarva-vedeshu shabdah khe paurusham nrishu

"I am the taste in water, O son of Kunti, and the radiance of the sun and the moon. I am the sacred syllable Om in the Vedic mantras; I am the sound in ether, and the ability in humans."

The word OM is used in prayer, before and after prayer, in yoga, while chanting mantras and in meditation.

Scientists have shown with research that Om chanting offers significant benefits to the activities of the brain, relaxation, metabolism, and overall well-being. Om is also a seed syllable used as a building block for many other mantras during meditation.

A lot has been written and spoken about Om. The word, meaning, its origin, the significance, the effects of Om chanting, the benefits, and other uses. I thought I have studied it all and now one only needs to apply the learning and the simplest way is to chant "Om".

Then I come across this book by my friend Nasir Zaidi, "Om: The Timeless Sound"; and I re-discover Om. Written in prose poetry form sprinkled with the timeless wisdom of the ancient sages and practical, doable advice, this book adds a new dimension to one's knowledge about Om.

The reader will personify the Om, feel connected and have a conversation with "Om". After reading it once, the book will serve as a ready reckoner, a guide that one can go to for any advice. Om is the Lord, Om is the friend, Om is divine.

Nasir is a skilled author and has been writing on several topics over the years now. With this book, he takes it several notches higher. In "Om: The Timeless Sound" he has compiled his knowledge, beliefs and all that he stands for. The book is a reflection of the persona that Nasir is. He uncovers for the reader all that he has become.

With "Om: The Timeless Sound", Nasir adds to more to the hundred meanings of Om. As a reader of this book, I am sure you will enjoy it and will want to go back to it time and again.

Here's wishing Nasir the best, and all his readers a joyous experience.

Dipan Vaishnav
Career Growth Coach, Assessor, Organization Designer

Author's Note

I was inspired to write ***Om: The Timeless Sound*** after reading Sri Aurobindo Ghosh's **Savitri.** In my opinion **Savitri** is a work of the highest order. A timeless classic. I have read **Savitri** twice and after reading every page, I would shake my head in sheer disbelief. How could someone come up with such a mind-blowing epic poem? Only a person whose intellect was spiritually inclined could have done so. It is difficult to say whether Sri Aurobindo Ghosh was a poet in a monk's garb or a monk in a poet's clothing but what I can say is that he was a scholar of supreme class, a philosopher of infinite wisdom and a poet who had complete mastery over symbolism, sound, syntax, structure and imagery.

I cannot claim to have understood **Savitri** wholly because to understand Sri Aurobindo Ghosh's thought one should be spiritually evolved. But in line after line, he raises the bar. He holds the reader spellbound. I am still under **Savitri's** spell, though considerable time has elapsed since even my second reading. So impressed was I by Sri Ghosh's **Savitri** that I searched for his collected works. In one of the volumes, I read about his impressions on Om:

Om is the syllable (the Imperishable); one should follow after it as the upward song (movement); for with Om one sings (goes) upwards;

Then in another volume I read,

Om is the mantra, the expressive sound-symbol of the Brahman Consciousness...the mantra Om should therefore lead towards the opening of the consciousness to the sight and feeling of the One

Consciousness in all material things, in the inner being & in the supraphysical world…

Before reading this, I knew of Om as the most basic mantra and that its recitation was a Hindu tradition. Sri Aurobindo Ghosh aroused my curiosity in Om with his profound thought and masterly writing. So much so, that I was compelled to express my own awareness and perception about Om.

Om is a virginal sound. The only sound that retains its virginity despite innumerable chanting since the world was created. The sweetest sound. The clearest sound. The most dynamic sound. The first sound. The original sound. The sound with multiple meanings. The sound that throbbed when there was nothing. The sound that makes the universe throb.

Om is not only a tool for meditation, as stated by various scholars. Om is a tool to understand Life. Om connects the self with the cosmic world. Om takes you beyond boundaries. Om resurrects. Om revives. Om rejuvenates. Om is the most sacred sound.

Every creation has an essence. Om is the essence of Krishna. Krishna is Om. Om is the essence of Shiva. Shiva is Om. Brahman is Supreme Self. The Creator of all existence. Om is Shabda Brahman (Brahman as sound).

Om is a rhythm, a beat that inspires. Om is soul's nourishment. The deeper you go in this sound, the stronger you emerge. Om is vibrancy. Om is energy. Om is universe's music. Om establishes a bond between the self and the Creator. Om transforms. Om renovates. Om penetrates.

Om is the soul of Gayatri Mantra, the most powerful mantra. Om bhur bhuvah suvah. When you chant this, you rise. You gain ascendancy. You soar towards the Ultimate. You reach the cosmic consciousness. You become one with the One.

Om, Om, Om, Om, Om.

Om is a shield. Om protects. Om fortifies. Om is the music of the heart, the lyrics of the soul. One should make Om rule the mind and let Om echo and re-echo in the being. Om should influence every action.

Submerge in this sound. Let the waves of Time roll over you.

The present, the past, and the future are indeed, Om. And whatever else is beyond these three dimensions of Time – that also is in Om.

In ***Om: The Timeless Sound***, I have attempted to convey through songs and verses my own ideas and views about Om, the most sacred mantra in the universe. Written mostly in free verse, there are some poems that follow the rhythmical pattern. At some places, Om talks to you in the first person and at other times, the focus is on its force and power and influence. The songs and verses are not inter-connected, though some are. The emphasis is on Lord Krishna but some verses extol the virtues of different mantras associated with other gods also.

I hope the readers enjoy reading the book and should any of them find that Om is misrepresented in any song or verse, I request that it is brought to my notice through my publisher, so that I stand corrected.

May the chanting of Om bring good luck to everyone.

Nasir Zaidi

1. When Nothing Was Nothing

I am timeless, I am immortal, I am forever.
I have no restrictions, I am free, I am always.
I sail on the imagination of the poets;
I live in the intellect of the philosophers.

No one knows the complete truth about me;
For many I am just a matter of conjecture.
Life without me is not possible;
With my exit, life extinguishes, yet
I survive even if life is not there.

I have a mind of my own, I have a life of my own,
Time means nothing to me, I am dimension-less.
I am the dawn of new life; I am the dusk of dying life.
I am in the universe and even beyond.
I know no boundaries; I know no barricades.

By chanting me, you can see infinity,
Why infinity, you can see beyond that,
You can hug the towering sky and play with the fiery sun;
You can toss the moon whenever you're in the mood.

The lotus of knowledge cannot bloom without me;
I make the fields of ignorance fertile.
I am a positive current; I am the much-needed blood.

When even nothing was *nothing*
I was breathing in the bubble of existence;
Somewhere in the heavens I had a presence,
Somewhere in the mind of the Creator I had a place.

I am my own identity; I am my own natural self,
Nothing can substitute me; nothing can replace me.
Eons have passed, eras have gone,
I remain as I was as I will.

I am the epicenter of the Universe;
The whole world revolves around me;
The wheels of fortune run on me.

I do not distinguish between black and white;
I do not discriminate between rich and poor.

I am the inspiration for the ones who can't breathe;
I am the motivator for life after death.
Vacant thoughts rule the mind of men;
They forget the purpose, the divine purpose, the goal.
To reign supreme is to obey the cosmic rule;
Here and there, a foot here, and a foot there,

Creates confusion, skepticism, a burning doubt.

The whole universe is in a flux, a continuous journey,
All come and go, while coming they take the baton, while
Going they give the baton to the successor.
There is no pause, no resting time, no stop-over,
Since the beginning this marathon is being run.

New runners replace the runners who fall by the wayside;
No one knows when this marathon will end.
End though, it never will, only the venue will change.

The marathon will continue just like it is now
But then the number of runners will remain the same;
The same runners will keep on running;
No one will fall by the wayside then, no one will tire.
The essence of eternity will be realised then;
While now it is only a word in the lexicon.

Men are strange creatures, portrait of contradictions;
They do not believe what they see many a time,
While they almost always believe what they do not see.
They have their own way of reasoning, own arguments.

Some among them attain the heights of Buddha;
Some among them remain at the lowest ladder.
Against all odds, some will fight to the finish;

Against trivial problems, many will succumb.
Life is shown scant respect by thousands of them;
While thousands more become devotees of life, worshippers.

The spiritual journey is just the starting point;
The end point becomes immaterial, the destination unimportant.
The journey itself is so breathtaking, so exciting,
That all else fades, recedes, becomes a blot, an insignificant dot.
Nirvana is attained when the mind is at peace with one self;
Peace is the prized possession, inner peace, a rare gem.
When the spirits are high, possibilities emerge;
When the spirits are low, the world appears dark.

Chant Om, Om, Om and feel the difference.

2. Krishna Is The Mind Of The Senses

Life shouldn't be casually thrown away;
But mortals are mortals they behave mortally;
Since the Beginning, men have behaved differently,
For many, everything is hogwash; to some, even stone is God.

He is the Maker, he is the Un-Maker, He is, He was;
He is the Absolute, He neither begets, nor is He begotten.
He is One, and yet He can be perceived in and around you.

All praise is for Him; He is the Master, the Commander.
Children of lesser gods denounce Him, deny Him.
But those who are enlightened know the truth;
Truth is obvious, visible, palpable, easily felt.
It cannot be denied even by blind men
But men do exactly that---they feel different.

Castigating the Supreme Being makes one feel superior;
It is a classic case of inferiority complex.
There is no cure for it save opening the eye;
But blind men are led by blind men;
The ditch is where they all fall into.

For some this world is a heavenly place, but for some,
The believers, the hard-core believers, this world is
A temptress out to seduce them to commit sins.
They guard themselves by prayer and self-abstemiousness,
And by singing Om, Om, Om.

I give them strength and power to deal with evil;
Of all, Desires are the most dangerous;
More dangerous than the most poisonous serpent,
More dreaded than the multi-hooded Kaliya.

To counter Kaliya, one has to be like Krishna.
He is the consciousness, the breath of the universe.
The blue-skinned god drives away blues;
He can make you reach the pinnacle of awareness.
He creates ways and paths for you for salvation.

Reflection on his name opens doors to secrets;
He is the centre; everyone and everything revolves round him.
He resurrects, He destructs, He guides, He delivers.

He *is*, he was always *is*, he is a world within a world,
He commands the cosmos; he is the mind and the mind is he.
Call him to kill the Kansa in your souls, tell Hari to hurry,
And set you free from the Kauravas in your minds;
He is the *daata*, he is the deity, he is the *swayam bhagwan*.

He is the energy, he is the power, he is the Divine Spirit;
Seek him to elevate your status, make you clean and chaste.
He is the magician, he is Nandlal, he creates magic.
When he plays the flute of enlightenment, he is Murli Murari,
He makes the soul dance, the spirits cavort, the mind waltz.
He transforms wildernesses into Vrindavan.

Krishna is the mind of the senses.

He is Bihari, Damodar, Ghanshyam, Giridar, Gopal, Govinda.
He is Jagannath, Kanhaiya, Keshav, Mahendra, Pandurang.
He is Rajagopal, Shyamsunder, Vasudev, Vishwatma, Yogeshwar.
He is the source of all spiritual and material worlds;
Everything emanates from him; nothing exists outside Krishna.

He is the dancing god, the blue deity, Arjuna's charioteer;
He is Mahabharata's chief architect, the master strategist.
He is Vishnu's eight avatar; he is the Lord of Dwarka;
He has hands like lotus and yet is formless.

Everything is because of his energy; he is the Supreme Lord.
He is a magnet that attracts all; he is the most beautiful.
He is the wealthiest and yet he is not attached to anything in this world.

When required he can relinquish his godhood status
And dance with the gopis; he transforms transformation.

Enigma, ecstasy, completeness, fulfilment, mysterious, powerful,
Mesmerizing, hypnotic; he is the lord of legends, the father of folklore.
He is the conscience in the heart of all the creatures.

He is music, magic, mantra. He is Manohar.
He has a thousand colours, each different than the other.

Say Jai Krishna, Jai Krishna, Jai Krishna,
Say Om, Om, Om, Om, Om.
Hari Om Hari Om…

3. Doubt Is A Killer

To be like Krishna, you have to change, transform;
Change doesn't happen on own- it has to be facilitated;
But man is an egoistic animal, he dislikes facilitators,
He wants to rule though he allows his ego to rule.
A bundle of contradictions, he is mostly confused;
When the world will blink for the last time
He will not know what has happened, he will simply cease.

The mornings and the nights are chasing each other
Like a romantic youth running after his beloved;
Time is galloping at an alarming pace like a startled stallion
But still an element of doubt hangs in the atmosphere;
This doubt is a killer, it knows no mercy;
It kills with utter ruthlessness plunging the knife deep in the heart.

Man should be careful about this dreaded assassin
But he throws caution to the wind and is careless;
Little time spent in chanting Om, Om, will help
But he doesn't like guidance of any form, of any kind;
When he is out of his mind, he will even climb mountain to seek God;
When he is saner, he won't even bother to say Om.

Life is so meaningful, so momentous, so significant,
Life is a gift so precious, so awesome;
Yet preference is given to insignificant things,
Importance is attached to irrelevant matters.

The world is not a damned place as many say;
The world is damned for the less deserving ones.
The ocean of life churns up surprises and shocks;
To dive in or to abstain is the individual's choice.
The more aggressive ones jump into it,
The scared ones turn back and flee.
The in-between ones stand at the edge and watch.

The ocean of life continues to flow steadily, quietly,
Like it has been continuously flowing since the dawn
Of the world, steadily, quietly, drowning those
Who couldn't adapt and learn to swim;
Reaching the daring ones to the shore of satisfaction
And passing by right under the nose of the in-between ones.

It changes its course for those who dare to live;
Living is acknowledging the existence of the Creator,
Otherwise, it is not living----merely existing.

The daredevils leave a blazing trail behind them;
They are the ones who have a mountain of faith in them.
Nothing can dislodge this monumental belief;

Swords and spears, arrows and stones, an army of millions
Make no difference to them, is of hardly any consequence;
These daredevils rely not on arms and ammunitions;
They are inspired by the surging love of the One and Only.

They chant Om, Om, Om, Om, Om;
They change the perception of Life forever.
When the connection with the Supreme Being happens,
The purpose of Life will slowly come to light.
Such a realisation drives away the darkness of the past;

Everyone has a Krishna in them but majority are oblivious of his presence.
They have neglected him for all these years, isolated him in one faraway corner
Of their hearts, where he sits, looking dazed, disturbed, and out of place.

To revive him they have to change their outlook, their view;
Krishna can show them the light but they have to see.
If they keep the eyes of their inner self shut, tightly closed
Then only the Supreme Being can help them, and He never will.
He wills only what He wills, not what others will.

The rightly guided ones are the enlightened ones;
They are Krishna themselves; they dazzle and shine

Like the lustrous stars on the dark, black sky,
Emanating rays that illuminate the darkest of minds.

4. Krishna & Kaliya

If all men have a Krishna in them, they all have a Kaliya in them too;
The struggle is between the staid Krishna and the sly Kaliya.
Though most of the time, the struggle is one-sided;
Still, there are occasions, when the quiet and serene Krishna
Destroys the Kaliya with a mere twinkle in his eye;
This twinkle in the eye is the glimpse of the mighty lord.

When eyes refuse to catch the glimpse of the Creator
Then Kaliya overpowers and rules the head and the mind.
So, it has been happening, and so it will happen,
Till the morning of eternity comes riding on the sun of deliverance;
Then there will be no more opportunities, no more chances;
Temporary life will become one with eternal life;
At last, fleeting hopes will fade away, and permanence, perpetuity
Will take over----the Lord would have delivered his promise!

Finally, the final days of this transient world will be set into motion;
The trumpet of doom will blow and a chain reaction will start.
Everything will disintegrate, the earth and the mountain,

The sky and the ocean, the sun and the moon, all living, non-living things.

A colossal emptiness will remain, a blob of nothingness
And this world would have passed into another world.
A world that is utopian in all respects, a perfect world.
No one has seen it so far but it has a universal appeal;
No transgressor will ever get to enter this world.
The mind gets numbed with this thought, stumped.
And a numbed mind, a flummoxed mind, loses its capacity.

Satan attacks such minds with a ferocity not seen anywhere;
He further cripples it and makes it dance to his tune
Like a drug-addict craving for his regular dose.

When he has these crippling minds under his control,
He sets them loose to influence other minds.
He has a huge army of zombies under his spell
And he is busy increasing the numbers, adding them up.
He has a mission to accomplish and he is focused.
He is ruthless, cunning, bold, and outrageous;
There are no rules for him to follow----it's an open field
And the Creator has given him complete freedom.

'Do whatever you want to do, mislead whomever you want to,

You are free to use any tactics you want, any tricks you can think of,
I will not stop you in your endeavour at all.
The world is yours to hoodwink, to create mischief
But remember one thing, those who have belief in me,
Those who know and understand me, those who trust me,
They will never get under your spell, their trust in me
Will act as a shield against all the weapons you have in your armoury.
They are the choicest ones, the distinguished ones,
They are my friends; they are the ones who will be welcomed
To Heaven, where luxuries never imagined, awaits them.'

And so, Satan continues to twist and turn the minds of people,
Sometimes with a sweet tongue, sometimes with a crooked thought,
Sometimes with a sublime touch, sometimes with grandeur,
Sometimes with piles of money, sometimes with a shapely figure,
Sometimes with a boost to the ego, sometimes with false promises,
And men succumb, give in, and surrender to his wizardry.

Till Doomsday he will be seducing mankind with his temptations,

The Doomsday will be a reprieve, a boon, for the faithful ones.
At last, the war will end, the struggle will cease,
The believers will get the reward for their persistence, their faith.

The Lord is just and fair and keeps his promises
And He has promised several things to the faithful ones,
When He will unveil the wonders that He has created for them,
Awestruck, the believers will look open-mouthed.
Imagination, howsoever wild and fertile, cannot fathom
What these wonders are and how they will look.

Towards a glorious ending the world is moving,
Leaving behind a trail of memorable events.
Anyone with the slightest of power is a candidate for claiming godhood
But the ones who have the real power,
They praise the Lord all the time, they never make such claims.
They are the ones who make the world go round,
Their presence is essential for the universe to survive.

They keep chanting Om, Om, Om all the time.

5. The Arc Of Life Will Become A Full Circle

What begins has to end, that's the law;
I can see the atheists lifting their eyebrows,
The intellectuals have a frown on their faces.
What am I talking about? They seem to think.
They dismiss my voice as a childish cry
But I know what I am talking about.

I am not talking any nonsense that I can think of;
I am stating facts and these facts can be known only to the clear-minded.
The ones with a nebulous, hazy vision will never understand;
They will only find faults with the beliefs and the thoughts
Of the ones for whom the Creator is of paramount importance;

Sailing on the boat of doubt will make life difficult,
Today or tomorrow, the arc of life will become a full circle.
The cobwebs of doubt have to be removed, cleaned up.
Else nothing will remain, except a dead mind;
And when the mind is dead, everything else is dead.
Why die before the actual death?

But perhaps dying while alive is a malady for which there is no cure;
It's all a mind game and most of the time the mind is allowed to win.

A fine morning can turn into a bloody evening;
The gentle sun may become a killer and all will be lost.
The tomorrow of today is just a fantasy of an over-fertile mind;
Some love living in glass houses, some love throwing stones.
The dead live on, the living ones are dead-like.
Tears are shed, breasts are beaten, emotions run high;
Whoever had to go has gone oblivious of what he has left behind,
Bitter facts are bitter hence they remain bitter.

The tongue is used to the sweetness of life
But life is not a jar of honey.

I am a free bird that flies on the wings of anticipation;
If ever I had to die, if ever, then there would be nothing.
Life would cease like a car running out of fuel.

The Almighty has made me immortal, hence the life.
Life owes its very existence to me.
But for me there would be nothing, just nothing,
Even what is inanimate has life in them,

The silent sturdy mountains speak about strength.

Life cruises along smoothly, efficiently, until
A barricade of death stops it without any remorse.
The flowers of hope bloom and then fade away;
The butterflies of expectation flit flirtatiously.

Mourners mourn the glorious past while the present slips away
Into a hole of desperation and frustration
Where flies of decay buzz songs of ruinous charm;
The nothingness of the lost time becomes an idyllic moment
And when such moments accumulate, life takes a new form,
A new shape, a new dimension, a new beginning.

In this beginning lies the future of man and his children;
Survival is not only about being fit but also about being mentally agile.
When man falters, he can still survive, but when he gives up
Then his only hope is the change in his attitude.
For some it's an impossible task but for some it's just a matter of adjustment;
No one knows when death will strike but all know that one day it will strike.

The angel of death is busy all the time and yet he loves his job.
Slowly but surely the world is headed towards emptiness;

The same emptiness from which it emerged one day;
Emptiness is the divine void that no one has seen.
Even Adam didn't see it---how could he
While lying in the cradle of uncertainty?

Uncertain times do not last forever;
The wind of change blows some time or the other,
Most of the time people are caught off guard
And the moment of truth expires
Like a fish breathing its last out of water.

During good times all seems good and rosy
But when times are bad then even the sunshine is darkness.
Death should be experienced once only,
Dying several times while living destroys the core being.
There is no fun in living then;
Life is for living, not dying.

The hand of luck rubs always the other way,
The wheel of fortune turns always the other way.
Whether it is summer or winter, there's no time to cry.
The spring of hope herald glad tidings
But man is lost in autumnal loneliness.

Loneliness in its entirety is not a bad state
But when loneliness becomes delirious,

Then it's time to bolt, run away from this turmoil.

Say Om, Om, Om, only Om, Om, Om.

6. Real Self

Waker, Dreamer, Deep Sleeper, Real You,
Know your Real Self, know who you are.

There is something cold about the fiery sun
And there is something warm about the cold moon;
The stars twinkle but the light is feeble.

The fireflies and glowworms put up a dazzling display;
When the mind and heart meet, it's a moment to cherish.
Such moments though are rare and becoming rarer,
At the crossroads of confusion, the mind attempts to speak
But the thought is incoherent, all muddled up
As if fragments of sky are falling on the ground
And part of the earth is lifting to touch the sky;
Whether it's a farce or whether it's a fact, no one knows,
The eyes of wisdom are blindfolded.

Next to nothing is an odd phrase but life is odder;
Odder for those who are odd themselves;
Otherwise, there's plenty to ruminate about,
For a while there seems gloom even in bloom
But that's the poison in the mind, the defect in the vision,

This poison plays havoc with the thought process.

The Buddha within keeps his eyes shut,
The solution to this predicament lies in Shiva's third eye.
The third eye is the sentry, the sentinel that keeps a watch;
If only man was aware of his third eye
But he doesn't even make proper use of his two eyes,
He looks at everything without seeing anything.

Man has become so accustomed to seeing, that he doesn't see,
He doesn't see he is falling; what he sees is that he is rising;
The rise is his fall, he misses this crucial point;
The real rising is in his fall; fall first to rise.

When in chaos you chant Om, Om, Om,
The commotion will turn into a splendid isolation.
Around you, divine spaces will get created,
Bliss will float in the air like ecstatic butterflies,
Into a nirvanic state will transform everything.

Nothingness contracts into *something-ness*,
In that *something-ness*,you will blend.
Identities lose their identity, all are one,
Everything becomes confined in a single capsule of Oneness.
Oneness is a divine experience, a unique occurrence,
There is no darkness of any kind, no blackness,
The experience is rich and velvety, translucent and lucid.

Light emanates from every corner, nook and cranny,
Whiteness flows like a pearly sea gurgling at the threshold of Divinity.

Silence like a giant iceberg prevails everywhere;
Nothing stirs, not the heart, nor the mind, nor the spirit.
It's a point of no return, there's no coming back;
Even beauty and purity fades, only the experience remains.
But this experience cannot be shared, it has to be felt,
All can achieve but only a few really do achieve.

Krishna does it through his dance, Buddha through his trance;
Adam did it through his piety, Noah did it through his humility;
Christ found it at the cross, Abraham felt it in the raging fire;
David sensed it in his hymns and Moses in his conversations.

The world is just a blur like the scenery seen from a running train;
Getting down from the train won't help---the sight cannot be captured.
Even the most arresting sights becomes boring after sometime;
The setting sun gives a message:
Life is a see saw, one side is zenith, the other, nadir;
Up today, down tomorrow, that's how life works.

Perception is a strange thing---it differs from individual to individual;
Riding on the horse of delusion comes hope,
People trip over one another to hug the rider.
When they fail to do so, they become hopeless,
That's when the real problem starts.

One has to be practical in life, think differently,
But most get washed away by the waves of pessimism
Though just behind them is the shore of optimism.

Life can be really cruel for the careless ones
But who cares? No one cares, no one bothers.
Precious moments are wasted away, spent carelessly,
The scissors of time snips away at the heart of faith.

What is left is nothing but a mutilated belief
Writhing in deep agony and on the verge of dying.
The ultimate loser is man and he has only himself to blame
But pointing a finger at others is a reflex action;
While pointing finger at your own self is tantamount to moving a mountain;
Only faith can move mountains: so, say Hari Om Hari.

7. The Story of Life Has Many Twists And Turns - 1

And so, the story of life moves on,
And so, it will continue, unless you take it in your own hands.
The climax will not change, howsoever skillfully you handle it,
But the contents can change; you can chart out your own destiny.
It's a peaceful journey if you are content with what you have;
If not, then it can be worse than hell, a raging inferno will engulf you
You neither can live nor die; you are neither here nor there.

Like a beast of burden trudging up a rough terrain,
You lead your life with loads and loads on your conscience,
Bells toll in the distance but they are too distant
To provide any comfort to the tired body and spirit;
Bells will toll for you too but you do not know when,
Until then the load has to be borne by the conscience.

Man is all flesh and bones and he has a spring of desire within him;

That spring never dries up, is always sparkling and brimming;
One by one he goes on fulfilling his desires,
His whole life goes away in just fulfilling the desires,
Having desires is not a sin, being under its spell is;
Don't be under Kaliya's spell, let Krishna break that spell.

When you get carried away then there is no hope,
You may well write your own obituary.
Obituaries are meant to be a lesson for others,
But who wants to take a leaf from other's books?
Experience may not necessarily be the best teacher.

Let the intellect do its job-but only the heart is overworked;
An overworked heart can be fatal for the individual.
Day in and day out it's the same story,
Though in reality the story maybe entirely different.

Monotony is a perception, a figment of the mind;
When the sun never tires spreading its rays every day,
When the ocean ceaselessly keeps on flowing,
When the mountains don't tire standing still,
When the air keeps on blowing without complaining,
Then why does life seem boring, monotonous?

The story of life has many twists and turns,
Even its dullest chapter has moments;
A perfect morning, for some, is most imperfect,

While an imperfect evening is perfect for some.

Imperfection is not something to feel sorry for;
Not aspiring for perfection is the perfect crime.
Till the heart breathes the sweet fragrant air
The clock in the mind will keep on ticking
But man has become so used to the tick tock
That he cares two hoots, he lets the ticking continue
In the end he ends up as a mental wreck.

Though he is unaware of his mental condition,
The psyche can bear innumerable atrocities;
The poor heart cannot; it is so tender and fragile
Like the gentle dew that clings to the tip of the petal
Gradually sliding towards its doom;
All is not well, though all should be well,
The wellness of a being depends on Om.

Life goes on, irrespective of peace, happiness, and contentment;
The world is like a seasoned prostitute who has all the tricks
Under her belt to beguile and mesmerise even the most pious ones,
Tread carefully for if you don't then more than dreams can be broken;
And broken dreams leave a scar on the face of memory.

The trial and tribulation of a scarred memory is difficult to chronicle;
The present doesn't forgive the past for its wrongdoings;
It takes its revenge by killing the future.

Only feeble sounds of regret knock at the door of expectation
But expectation is deaf to all sounds;
The only sound that is meaningful is the silence of the consciousness.
Everything else floats in an illusory world, unknown to the self,
Knowing the self is a cosmic reality that cannot be proved false;
No matter how hard one tries, no matter how desperate he is,
There is no way in which he can trample upon the cosmic truth.

The Supreme Being has his own ways to tackle situations.
Remember, all situations change, now or after, but they all change.
What doesn't change is the mercy and kindness that flows from the Lord;
There is no end to it; it's like an ever flowing, everlasting river,
Yet many unfortunate ones fail to take a dip in it;
They prefer to swim in a pool of sin with sinners—the attraction is more there.

The razzmatazz always attracts----it's like a man hungering after an exposed nipple.

Forbidden territory is the first place that is likely to be explored;
But the exploration of the mind and the soul and the heart and the spirit
Like a lame leper in the corner of the street, is neglected,
Some who dare to be different - dare to be only slightly different -
Rush where even the angels fear to tread, not realising that
Within the self is a pot of gold waiting to be discovered.

Om, Om, Om, that's the only way to conquer.

8. The Story of Life Has Many Twists And Turns - 2

But worldly treasures tempt them more like a well laid out buffet table,
Yet they remain unsatiated even after stuffing their stomach with all kinds of foods.
The thirst for more doesn't get quenched, in fact it intensifies
Like the never-ending orgasmic desires of a nymphomaniac.
There is no cure, no prescription and no drug to stall this vice;
Virtue doesn't grow on trees or blossom like a flower,
It has to be cultivated, grown within you and honed by the knife of sacrifice.

Sacrifice is not only about slaughtering animals or donating gold;
It's about the struggle that one has to undertake against his own self.
You have to constantly fight with your inner self;
The self that holds more temptations than a virgin nautch girl,
The self that can break the piety of even the most pious person,

This very self can also give an individual, godhood.

It is how the self is managed, controlled, reined in;
Life can be hell or heaven depending on whose side you are.
If the world is heaven for you, life could be hell, then.
And if the world is hell for you, then life could be heaven.

Satan aspires to be God but cannot be God;
Sometimes he attains the garb of a holy man
Fooling the innocent and himself but the Almighty knows his ploy
Yet God lets him display his power and influence.

An ant cannot become an elephant and an elephant cannot become a palm tree,
The palm tree cannot touch the sky, the sky cannot be infinite.
Infinity boggles the imagination but the imagination has more powers;
It can outrun, outthink and outdistance infinity,
What has to end, ends, but what is immortal, endures.

Om, Om, Om, keep chanting Om, Om, Om.

The frightening aspect of life is its unpredictability
But that precisely is why life is so unpredictable;
Death stalks at every breath, like an invisible shadow it follows you everywhere.

The silence is loud and clear and the sound is deep and dense;
The woods of pretense create a chilling picture.

Death's shadow lengthens every moment, life shrinks.
As life melts, desire increases, passion runs high,
At the pinnacle stands death with arms spread to welcome you;
At the abyss death stands with outstretched arms to hold you.

You can escape everything, run away from everything, even from yourself
But death like a contract killer on the loose doesn't spare you;
That's the beauty of life, despite the terrifying presence of death,
It continues to flourish, bloom, like new flowers every day;
So let not the flower within you wilt and die.

Let it blossom and spread the fragrance of love to one and all,
What is left behind is only the footprint of memories
And these memories act like the tender hand of a mother
On the face of a baby putting her to sleep,
Especially when barbs of taunt pierce and prick the flesh;
The soothing remembrance of memorable events comforts it.

Look around, there are threads of memories to be picked up.
Do not get entangled in the mess of morbidity,
When you smell the flower of hope, you feel dynamic,

When you inhale the air of optimism, you feel strong,
That's the way to forge ahead, to make progress.

The world is a dreamy place but you got to be a dreamer;
Otherwise, dreams are like fragile glasses kept at the edge of a table,
Any moment the glasses can slide to their glassy death;
When dreams shatter, the fragments penetrate even the thickest of skin,
Leave alone, a tender, soft, fragile, babyish heart that bleeds
Like an accident victim on a busy highway hit by a 6-ton trailer.

Sometimes it's too late to make a comeback- it's the point of no return.
You are nowhere; there is nothing left for you, absolutely nothing,
Only realisation of the folly can still provide a slim chance
To make amends with time that has been wronged by you,
There is nothing more dangerous than scorned time.
It is a great leveler like death and swiftly does justice.
The king sits on the throne but where is his crown?
The commander wins the battle but has lost the war,
Love throbs in the heart but the sweetheart is already married.
Life becomes a mirror of paradoxes.

In the air hangs the tale of pain and regret

And that's the sorriest thing that can happen to any individual;
The world passes by like a canoe adrift on the swirling river.
Turn to Krishna for he is the one who can take you to shore,
Your hands are Krishna, your mind is Krishna and your thoughts are Krishna
But only when you free yourself from worldly affairs.

Om, Om, Om, say Om, Om all the time.

9. A Divine Pause

When the mind is shackled and the body is free, there is no hope.
The bridge to connect people's heart is under-used;
As days transform into night and night changes into day,
Time runs, tirelessly, towards the end-line, with no competition.

For the brave, time is just a better athlete, but for the timid, time is a killer;
Huxley's brave new world has little takers, the world has moved on.
From the window of expectation can be seen a thread of hope,
It is all about willingness and the passion to conquer.
Conquering the world like Alexander isn't a strenuous task;
But to conquer the wicked mind, the evil thought, is like forcing a flaccid penis to become erect.

Where the mind falls asleep, the heart stays awake,
And where the heart sleeps, the mind is awake;
Better they both are asleep; the burden would be offloaded.
But if and when they both are awake, then the first flash of enlightenment happens.

That's the initial opening, the first awakening, the path to glory,
Success is not about winning; it is about not wanting to lose.
That's where the hare and the tortoise differed.

I am not a preacher, I do not like preaching, I like to state facts,
And facts can be cruel, ruthless, bitter, and uncomfortable.
The cloak of fear has to be discarded, thrown away in the bin.
When the cool rain falls on the parched earth,
It is an orgasmic joy, the apex of satisfaction, but
It is not a state of statelessness -
The state of statelessness propels the individual to unheard of level,
He is alone there; the silence is as deep as the ocean.
There is no light, no darkness, it's a strange world.

Like life's beautiful dreamy song, the music of the heart plays,
The tuneful melody stirs every pore of the body.
Dusk and dawn are intertwined, time is a stranger.
Black and white are unknown, there are no doors and walls;
Eliot's hollow men have no place here; they are fit only to be scarecrows.
In the faint glow that comes and goes of its own, an image emerges
And everything blends with it; the river of purity begins to flow.

For a while there is a pause, a divine pause that sends a ripple
Across space and the cosmic world throbs, palpitates,
The world takes a breather, the shivery feeling tantalises,
Those who believe, have faith, they absorb the experience,
For others, this earth-shattering event never happened.

To choose between two paths is easy but to walk on the chosen path is tough;
But walk we must, for if we remain stationary, the world will pass us by.
And it's a mad world; there is a mad rush, mad scramble for one-upmanship
But we have to choose between the mad race and the gentle walk.

If we don't choose, we will regret and that is the sore point,
A sore heart can still be nursed but a sore soul has no cure.
Time, like a sprinter in a 100m race, sprints away,
We are left clutching at our own egos.

Wait a minute, don't get me wrong; I have no enmity with ego;
We do not see eye to eye with each other but that's a different matter.
Memories get erased like a child erasing his doodles from his sketchbook.

The notebook of life lies untouched, unread, somewhere in the depths
Of the darkest corner of the heart
And in this way life goes on....

The strains of a wrecked heart awaken the dying spirits
And yet it is like sleeping with nightmares;
The scream that resonates of a blank wall
Makes the wall look bleaker and blanker,
Eyes though still stare at it as if it is a big-bosomed woman,
For how long will the mind not think? How long?
At some point, even the mountains erode,
But why wait until that long?

There are questions and then there are more questions
But where are the answers? And where is the conviction?
Is there a place where they can be searched? Is there?
If only this could be known—but how?

Knowing isn't a task that one can learn,
Knowing comes only with experience but not all experiences.

The heart has to listen, the mind has to speak,
Quietly life ebbs away like a dying man's last moments;
We stand and watch while the movie of life starts and ends,
Sometimes we react a bit too late and sometimes we don't.

Reactions are like stale sticky noodles that have no taste,
The soul needs vacuuming and the mind cleaning,
But we don't like to do chores ourselves, we like to order, command,
Precious minutes tick by and we end up throwing the clock against the wall,
The journey ends before it really starts.

Om, Om, Om. Only Om, Om, Om.

10. Life Is A Strange Paradox

Man has something that he doesn't want to lose
And yet he strives to gain more and more,
The crux of the matter is that there is no matter.
Something works for someone and someone works for something,
Life is a strange paradox
To those who only wander and wonder,
Life is more than a string of events
But why wander to wonder?

The external light extinguishes but the illumination within, doesn't.
Why be afraid of darkness? Why be afraid of anything at all?
Life plays the song that you want to hear
So why choose sorrowful lyrics?
If the painter of your mind paints a picture of pathos
Then it is you who should take the blame?
The world is merely a spectator,
It will clap when you perform,
It will boo when you don't.
But alas! The joys of memories are short-lived.
Bury the hatchet, bury the past.

Welcome today as if there was no yesterday and there is no tomorrow.

Chant Om, Om, Om and again chant Om, Om, Om.

When you close your eyes, what do you see?
When you open your eyes, what do you not see?
Philosophy has got nothing to do with how you want to lead your life;
Life is not only about joy and sorrow,
They come and go like autumn and spring,
Don't make life seasonal—life is beyond that.
In a jiffy life can be snuffed out- we all know that,
For the marathoner, the last strides are of utmost importance.

From here, there, but from there, where? The mystery deepens.
The day will end and another will begin,
Who says monotony has no excitement?

The unexpected has strange ways of landing at your doorstep;
Behind closed doors, nothing happens.
And when something does happen, the door remains closed,
Life carries on with minimum fuss, with the same alacrity.

But when someone gets lost in the darkness of his own soul
Then no light can show him the way;

Dante's purgatory maybe a better place to live in.

When the moon looks like the sad face of an orphan
And the stars around it twinkle like rich brats taunting
Then you'll be faced with a tricky dilemma
To be like the moon or like the stars?

If you are a stranger to your own self,
You can't hope to become friends with others.
When the mirror of your identity cracks, the splinters will scatter,
In each minuscule glass, you'll see an unknown face.

Existence crawls on like a snail in a 100metre dash;
The earth whispers something that you cannot catch,
Don't become deaf to the sounds of nature.

Pagodas of disbelief will appear within you,
Temples of doom will emerge around you,
Om, Om, Om is the only way out, so say Om.

Life is not doubt; life is not a magician's trick.
Life is wonder; life is magic itself.

Nothing changes; nothing changes when you don't want to,
But when you want to, then you can lift a mountain on your little finger,

Then you can expand your body into 16108 forms,
Then you can display the whole universe in your mouth,
Then you can transform a hunchbacked woman into a beauty.

Krishna, Krishna, say Jai, Jai Krishna.

If you sit like a statue, then only birds will shit on you
And dust will accumulate thick and fast;
Soon, you will resemble a relic of a hoary past,
And past and present have always fought over the future.
When the momentous occasion will arrive,
The past, the present, and the future will not matter.

With your inner eye see Arjuna's chariot riding into the sunset
But Krishna's image appears at every sunrise.

Om Shanti Om, Shanti, Shanti, Om.

11. Awaken The Mind, Free Your Soul

Awaken the mind, free your soul,
Stop living in a world of confinement.
You only can help yourself, no one else will,
Come out of the cover of darkness,
Witness the light that shines brilliantly,
If you see deep within, you'll know its source.

The world is not a fiction and neither are you,
But the fact is that you aren't aware of the facts.
What you know and what you don't know,
The difference between the two is unknown to you.
Closed mind is not the culprit, the culprit is
Your unwillingness to liberate your thoughts.

Peace, peace, peace, welcome it in your life,
Settle the differences you have with your soul.
Fly in the cosmic world, soar in the worlds beyond it,
Sing the song of life, hum the tune of tranquility.
Become one with your own self, get into the groove,
If you wish to merge with the One, merge within first.

Om Hari Om, Om Hari Om, Om Hari Om,

Let this sound throughout your body roam.
Secrets that are locked in secrets will unravel,
To lofty and sacred places your mind will travel.
Your thoughts will become cleaner, purer,
Your steps will become steadier, surer.

When what is in you is set free, what is left in you.
If you knew it, you wouldn't believe, so what's the use?
This is That or I am That or All is That, imagine,
Redefine your being to dip into the Being.
The opportunities are plenty but there's less time;
In every dimension you'll find me, there's nowhere,
Where I am not there, I am everywhere, here or there.

Caress your soul with my chant, make it alive,
A befuddled mind is a sorcerer's weapon to destroy.
Whatever you think you are, whatever you think you aren't,
There's a thin line that divides the two opposites.
Tread confidently but with soft little steps,
For any sound that you make will break the spell.

Be the one who creates a spell, be like the blue-god;
The permanent among the impermanent; the unique,
He discards desires and releases you from all ties,
No need to invite him in your heart, he is already there,
Awaken to his presence, become aware of his existence.

How can you exist if you deny his existence? Think.
He is a thinker who makes all thinkers wonder,
He is all-making, all-knowing, he is owner of all,
He is the source, he is the self, he is the source of the self,
He rules the universe, he is the protector, he is omnipresent.

Om Hari Om, Hari Om Hari, dance to his tunes
And the world will dance to your tunes, let Krishna music
Overflow from every pore of your body, surrender
Yourself to his magnificence, his brilliance, his supremacy,
He is the basis of everything, everything is because of him.

He is abundance, his abundance is limitless, so
Expand your thought, stretch your imagination,
Elevate yourself by thinking of him, accept who you are,
Accept what he is, let there be no conflict, he is the Super-soul.
He is the moon among the stars, of all lights, he is the sun,
He is effulgent, he is effervescent, he is energetic.

No one knows his origin, no one can know his origin,
Know that he is the beginning, but he is beginningless,
Know that he is the form, but he is formless,
If you attain Krishna consciousness, then it's a nirvanic state;
Nothing to reject, nothing to accept, you are above all this.

Jai Krishna, Jai Krishna, Jai, Jai Krishna,

12. Become The Buddha Of Your Own Self

The walls of doubt will never collapse on its own,
Unless the uncertainties implode within you;
Once you are surrounded in the debris of your skepticism,
The explosion outside will occur at once, in a jiffy.

Cleanse your soul by inhaling Krishna, he is the fragrance;
Make your life aromatic, so scented and perfumed that no odor,
No stench, no stink or reek or any whiff of foul smell remains.

Don't apply logic with him, he is the universal truth.
He is the splendor in splendid, the fineness in fine,
He is the wonder in wonderful, the greatness in great,
He is the strength in strong, the intellect in wise,
He is intelligence, wisdom, virility, power and wealth.

Om Hari Om, say it from the inner depths of yourself,
Delve deep into your soul and chant his name, slowly,
Let the aura of him engulf you, let his radiance drown you,
Let his calmness calm you, let his sweetness sweeten you,
Embrace him and you embrace the heaven and the earth.

Om is the sound, Om is the word, Om is the tongue,
Om is the language, Om is the dialect, Om is the accent,
Om is the pronunciation, Om is the grammar, Om is the speech,
Om is what you hear, Om is what you speak, Om is Om.

Go beyond every boundary, scale every hill of limitation,
Wade through the high tide of disasters in your life,
Pluck flowers from barren trees, dig wells in parched lands,
Make miracles the way of your life, work wonders every moment,
Conquer all disbeliefs, banish all negativity, welcome Krishna.

Let him dance away the negativity from your life, he is the Great Dancer;
The whole universe dances when he dances, he is *sat-chit-ananda vigraha*;
The distance between the Brahman and the soul vanishes, let him dance,
Let the splendour of his dance penetrate your innermost being,
Let your spirt and the soul and the heart and the mind dance with him,
Glory is for those who surrender to him, so submit yourself wholly.

O Krishna, Krishna, O Krishna, Jai Krishna, Jai Krishna, Jai

Krishna.

He will suck away the poison from the breast of evil, so,
Be not afraid of the Putanas in your life,
Worship him the way you want, in the form you wish,
You will obtain deliverance, that's his promise to mankind.
Call Kesav to slay the many Kesins who have surrounded you,
Make him a habit, an everyday ritual, and see how life transforms.

Take shelter in him to attain the ultimate destination,
Engage the mind, establish the connect with him,
Get absorbed in him, worship him, he is the controller, the supreme master.

He is the sacred abode, the eternal, the transcendental, the original,
He is the unborn and yet he is, he is mystical, mystic, mystery,
He has no symmetry and yet is perfect symmetry, he is limitless,
His opulence exceeds all limitations, he is the most perfect.

Desire him and you will never desire anyone or anything else;
He fulfills all expectations, all needs, all wants, all you can imagine,
Focus on him, he is the only Focus, think of him, nothing else to think after that.

Shut your eyes and see his divine image, open them and hug his presence,
The world will be at your feet if you prostrate at his feet,
Make him the supreme goal of your life and attain nirvana.

Become the Buddha of your own self, say Krishna, Krishna.

13. Do Krishna-Karma

In the swampy mess of your life, make a lotus bloom,
Look into the lotus eyes of Sri Krishna and dispel the gloom.
Whatever you wish to see, you will behold in his holy form,
But for that you need to usher in a change, so transform.

The mind is the villain, don't let it persecute you,
If you allow it to, then what you see won't be the real view.
So, detach from all attachments, break free from all constraints,
Become one of the pictures that Krishna's presence paints.

Drink the water to taste him, look at the sun to see his light,
And in the moon, you'll see him shining when it is night,
You can escape all predicaments of life if you only think him,
He is the idea, the concept, the thrill, the fancy, and the whim.

Make music with his *bansuri*, with his *chakra* slay inner devil,
Become beautiful with his *morpankh*, with his *gada* kill all evil,
Herald glad tidings with his *shankh*, with his *sharanga* hit the target,

Weave him in your life so that you can weave your magic carpet.

Imagine him, not how he is, for who can ever sketch his image,
He is goodness personified, every pore of his is a place of pilgrimage,
Worship him with your eyes and mind and experience enlightenment,
Instantly the soul will be cleansed, purified will become the environment.

Hail him, cherish him, sing him, breathe him, love him all the time,
Make him the reason of your life and your life forever will be in its prime.
So, Krishna-karma is what you do; all your actions only to please him,
Dazzling brilliance will overshadow all that is pale, dull, hazy and dim.

The ocean of birth and death is nothing but Krishna, and Krishna only
Can rescue you from any situation, he is your friend when you're lonely,
Have only one desire and that to attain him, for if you attain him,

Your glass of fulfilment will always be filled up to the brim.

He lives in everyone's heart but not all live in his heart, for that
Fix your mind only on him and every moment with him chat,
Take the *bhakti-marg* and from *samsara* you will gain freedom,
That's the glorious path, that's what gives the wise, wisdom.

Be balanced in joy and sorrow, be tolerant, and be egoless, selfless,
Strive not for any fruits but keep working and Krishna will bless,
Enter the silence zone and stay there forever, for silence is divine,
All impurities and vulgarities and the bad in you, Krishna will refine.

So, chant Hare Krishna, Hare Krishna, Krishna Krishna, Hare Hare
He is the beloved, he is the love, so keep longing for Murari *pyaare*.

14. Float In the Spiritual Sky

Eternal life awaits you; immortality beckons you,
The world is only a chimera, come out from the illusion.
Scan the horizon and see Krishna stretched everywhere;
What you *are* and what you can *be* depends on now, not next.

From being a bush, you can tower as an undying banyan tree,
All parts of yours will then sing Vedic hymns, Puranic psalms,
You'll float in the spiritual sky where there's no sun and moon,
You'll be the sun, you'll be the moon, you'll be the Milky Way;
So, emerge from the darkness and become self-luminous.

The foolish know not what they are missing,
What they have missed, what they'll miss,
To them nothing means nothing, but to the enlightened one,
Nothing is everything and in this everything is nothing.

Bend the mind like Krishna split up Shiva's bow like a dry leaf;
Don't live, be the juice of life, become Life itself.
Convert your mindscape into Krishnascape to catch a glimpse of him;
He is the wisest sage, the greatest teacher, he is knowledge itself,

From him emanates all learning, all philosophy, all spirituality.

Swim effortlessly in the pool of tranquility, listen to the ripple,
The sound that you hear is Om and if you listen ever carefully,
You'll hear Om again and again Om and Om and only Om,
Let this sound run in your blood and in your body roam,
Softly say Om, loudly speak Om, then in the silence hear Om.
Become blissfully aware with Om, become blissfully unaware with Om,
Let this sound rule your conscience, let your consciousness echo Om,
When the heart whispers Om, when the soul sings Om, when Om
Is the only sound that you hear and utter and it sinks into your every pore,
When Om stirs your inner being and your inner being awakens,
You will find a spot in the core of Krishna, in his innermost self.
The ways to damnation are many, the way to salvation is only one;
Through *saranagati* attain *moksha*, Krishna will be the catalyst,
Know your *self* first before you know the Unknown, peep inside;
Your soul is your parent and your child too, your sibling and spouse, too.

Hoping to live and livingly living makes hell of a difference in heavenly living,

The days are brighter when you smile, the nights are darker when you brood.

If you don't uplift yourself, Krishna won't; but if you, then he'll elevate you.

Ignorance maybe a curse but emptiness of the mind is definitely not,

So, empty it fully, let out all that is in, all, make it emptier than emptiness.

An empty mind is like a new-born baby; fresh, raw, innocent, accepting,

Ever-new Joy is Krishna, he is irresistible, so don't try resisting him.

When the world tries to seduce you, see Mukunda's smiling face,

Get seduced by that curve, he'll set things straight for you, if you so wish.

His infectious smile will infect you and make you sail through hail and storm.

If you realise you are self-realised, that's something else, not self-realisation;

It's like if you think you are humble, you aren't, that's your ego talking.

That body is not yours, that mind is not yours, and neither is the soul yours,

You neither control your birth nor your death and yet your feet is not grounded;
Trance-like state can be attained only if you are purified by intelligence.
The more you think you *are,* the more you *aren't,* you *aren't* what you *are,*
Shed the image you carry of yourself, it's excess baggage that's of no use,
Free yourself from yourself first before you seek what you are seeking;
Rise with Om, float with Om, fly with Om, explore the universe with Om.

15. Immerse In Krishna

Freedom from reaction is the ultimate freedom you can hope for;
Immerse in Krishna, for he only can make a *nar*, a Narayan.
Crush your *karma* and see life transforming around you,
To find the path of liberation is difficult, but not impossible,
Anyone can aspire to be the pure soul, but the Pure Soul is only one.

Every moment can be a treasure or a bite from a venomous serpent;
You decide whether you want the bounty or the snake's toxic sting.
Within you is the potential to smash a mountain into smithereens;
No one knows the Ultimate Reality but you belong to the Ultimate Reality,
Behind the Door of Secret is Krishna, the key to unlock it is Krishna.

Krishna is the revealer of secret, Krishna is the secret, with his aid
Climb any mountain, cross any river, change wilderness into an oasis;

To be firm and free from uncertainty, listen to the whispers of the soul.
Om it says, say Om, say Om, and when you chant Om, you find elevation;
From the pinnacle when you survey the scene, you'll see the dance of life.

Director of the dance of life is *natkhat* Natwar, so cling to him, hold on to him,
Rejoice in his presence, make every moment of your life joyous, donate joy.
Om is joy, joy is Om, Om is bliss, bliss is Om, bask in the warmth of Om;
To dispel the coldness of life and death and to set yourself free from *moh*,
Om Hari Om Hari Om Hari Om, Om Hari Om Hari Om Hari Om.

16. Become Krishna's Dancer

From earth embark on the odyssey of heaven, go wherever you wish,

No one can stop you, only you can be the obstacle, so no excuse.

You are your own master, your own teacher, your own philosopher,

Life is not life unless you know and death is not death unless you know.

Life is eternal, continuous; if that is so, then what is death?

Take refuge in Krishna, and death will never worry you, for there's no death;

Just the passing away of the soul is not death, ask Krishna, for no one dies, he says.

Who knows what Krishna knows; no one, so silently hear him out, he speaks

When you speak to him, he responds when you question him, he gives when you ask.

He is Ananta, Varuja, Aryama, and Yama, the lord of death, so he knows death

As he knows life and as he knows the heaven and the earth and the whole universe.

Strength, fame, wealth, knowledge, beauty, renunciation, Krishna displays all,
Beyond all relative truth there is an Absolute Truth; don't lose sight of it.

Sarva karana karanam
Bahunaa janmanam ante
Jianavan maa prapadyate
Vasudevau sarvam iti
Sa mahatma su-durlabhau

Remember the source and you will forever be on the path of enlightenment;
If you forget the source, you won't even remember your name, identity,
It's all about Krishna, it's all about him, around him, above him, below him.

The world is agog, there is expectation, the universe boss is present everywhere;
You can smell him, taste him, feel him, see him, hear him, he towers above all;
Your senses are not yours; they are his, you are a puppet, he is the Puppeteer.

If Krishna is your saviour, who can destroy you; if he destroys you, who can save you?

Make moments into memories, make memories into meditation, meditate on him;
Move your mind, stir your soul, shake your spirit, become the dancer of Krishna.
Do only to please him, live only to satisfy him, die only to delight him, say Om,
Om, Om, Om, let only one sound emanate from everywhere, Om, Om, Om.

17. Kiss Krishna's Lotus Feet

Mysteries surrounding you will unravel if you seek Krishna;
The end is endless, don't get beguiled by it, be bewitched by him.
The one who has knowledge of the beginning and the end and is
Eternal, ageless, perennial, permanent, forever, abiding, endless,
He makes life worth living and death worth dying, so become
His captive, let go off frivolity, and all that is unworthy and dubious,
Kiss his lotus feet and fountain of knowledge will sprout in you.

The way to fulfilment is Om, Om is the path to enlightenment;
Om elevates you, raises your stature, status and standing.
Inhale Om, exhale Om, while awake say Om, in dream recite Om,
Om is energy that gives energy to energy, so gain energy with Om.

Positive energy will take you closer and closer to the Supreme

Being,
Where there is no gap between the supplicant and the Great Giver,
Om, Om, Om, Krishna, Krishna, Krishna, Om Hari Om.

Ugly becomes beautiful, beautiful gets rosier, rosier turns into divine,
Touch a human's heart and you touch Krishna's overflowing bosom.
The days and nights fall into a rhythm and that rhythm is Krishna;
Solace you get, peace of mind, steadiness, and your soul gets richer,
No wealth can replace that experience and that experience is enriching.

Being lost in Krishna is a nirvanic peak, so bend to blend, submit to rise,
With Krishna rule your mind and whatever comes in and goes out of it;
Seal your lips not your heart, open your mind not your tongue, be patient;
What you lose for Krishna makes you spiritually wealthier, so gain that,
Gain limitless knowledge, unlimited wisdom, and perpetual intelligence.

Attain Om, retain Om, accept Om, awaken, arise, become aware,
Spur yourself with Om, inspire your intellect with Om, sing Om,
Listen Om, bask in its warmth, submerge in it, stick to it, surpass with Om.
Explore the world within you, discover the worlds within this world, say Om.
The primordial sound from which all sounds emerged, the mother of all sounds;
Recite in darkness to get light, recite in light to get informed, keep reciting
To get enlightened, when enlightened, recite more to reach a blissful state,
In blissful state recite to gain Buddha-hood, and as a Buddha when you say Om,
You cross over to the other side of the Veil, where, there is no *where*, nowhere,
A climactic state, selfless, formless, endless, and enduringly permanent;
Where even infinity takes a backseat and eternity seems like only a moment.

Tread on the souls of free men, embrace the burning sun, swallow the sky,
The whole universe is in you but you spend time looking over your shoulder.

Hum Om, revel in the sound, and then fall silent, in the vacuum echoes Om,
Piercing, penetrating, gripping, lyrically tempting, stimulating, energising,
Over hills and vales and dense forests, in green fields, seas and deserts,
Here, there, everywhere, on earth, in cosmos, beyond boundaries, Om vibrates.

18. Hari Om

Whiteness of soul provides illumination in times of darkness;
Kill the dark in you, light the lamp of love of Lord Krishna.
The ache that Radha had for him, the song that Mira sang for him,
Create a magical atmosphere, *aisi laagi lagan, Mira ho gai magan.*
Radhakrishna, the symbol of divine love, merge with the deity,
Love has no substitute; love is a celestial potion for immortality;
Get drunk on the blue-god, become a new you, an avatar.

Where not you can reach, it is all within your reach, reach for him,
See the change it brings in you and in life around you, become intimate.
Between nothingness and something-ness, there is a river of temptation,
Cross it with the boat of Om, oar of Om, sail of Om and the wind of Om.
Be not like the castaway on the shore of Desire, be the boatman of serendipity.

Alter the cosmic destiny, Krishna is the difference between man and superman;
Pause Time as you wish, retrieve moments from seconds, break the routine,
Convert adversity into opportunity, make night into day, say Om, Om, Om.
Flirt with eternity, become its eternal child, swing in the arms of infinity,
When it is hard to be strong, be soft to be strong, be flexible to be rigid;
Ride on the wings of Om, set your soul free, let it flutter and flap and fly and flip,
With Krishna on your lips dive into the well of unwell and make it a wellness well.

Hari Om is the mantra, Hari is the *mann,* Om is the *tra* or the transport,
Scale new heights, climb newer heights, soar into a dimensionless world;
Abandon yourself to find yourself, lose yourself to win yourself,
Shrink yourself to expand yourself, empty yourself to fill yourself,
This can become that, that can become this, you can become You;
The cosmos will kiss you; the earth will lift you, sing Krishna, croon Om

19. Om Creates A Spell

Words are silhouette of ideas; they are like man and his shadow,
For Ishwar there are plenty of words, but in Om, Ishwar is manifested.
So, Om it is and Om it was, and Om it will be, and Om surrounds us,
Destroy the seeds of past actions, for if you don't, they'll grow into
Huge trees, each with a thousand branches, that'll have a strangle hold
On you and your thoughts and your life will be a hellhole of suffering.

Realisation is the real thing; all the rest is only a preparation for it;
You may walk miles but reach nowhere and keep getting lost,
While you maybe stationary and yet complete a journey of a lifetime.
You cannot perceive God and Soul by external senses, you cannot,
To not relent when the writing is on the wall is a case of foolhardiness,

Write your own stuff, create a masterpiece, make your life legendary.

Legends are not born, legends are fashioned by Krishna, make Om an anthem;
An anthem for your heart, mind, soul and all that is in and out of you,
Leave reason behind, don't run after logic, faith can bolster your spirits,
Hold on to Krishna, let go off of everything else, flow with the present;
Inside you is not only you, drive away whatever is housed in it, and also you,
The sky is not the end; there are worlds beyond it, you can witness all
When you look inside Krishna's mouth, you'll see the whole universe.

Thinking makes, thinking destroys, think what thoughts you're thinking;
Thoughts shouldn't rule you, thoughts shouldn't be ruled by you;
Neither a slave nor a master be of your mind, both are ways to disaster,
Across the black silence runs a white line of sound, clasp that line,

Then enter a huge vacuum where only Om flows, flow with the sound.

Play with Krishna, don't play games with people and their hearts;
In the game of life and death, he is the Ace that can make you a winner.
Win his heart, woo him, please and satisfy him, live and die for him,
The world is an oyster and you are the pearl but don't get drunk on this
For Krishna is the oyster maker as well as the pearl maker,
He is the Ultimate Maker, so get made by him again and again and again.

If Krishna is your companion, then your steps will have a spring,
Even the worst autumn in your life will look as if it is spring,
The dry and parched patches in your soul will turn into spring,
From everywhere all glad and good tidings at you will spring.

Om does the trick, Om does the magic, Om creates a spell.

20. Waltz With Om

Waltz with Om in the spiritual playground
And in the divine space, create your own space.
Be a dawn in your life every day, a fresh morning,
Change the duskiness into radiant brilliance,
Be conscious of the Perfect, the Flawless Form,
Churn the milk of hope into a yogurt of gift.
Om, Om, Om, it is only Om, Om, Om.

Capture the kingdom of stars, sit on your own throne,
Be the king of kings, a royal of royals, noble, stately,
Bring the heaven at your feet, sit at Krishna's feet.
Gaze imploringly in his eyes and see the Unseen,
In the vast emptiness, in the great void, you'll witness
A magnificent magnificence that defies definition.
Om, Om, Om, it is only Om, Om, Om.

Don't be bogged down by the Immensity, be a warrior,
Scorch the sun with the blazing intensity in your soul.
When you fall, fall only in Krishna's lap, then leap
From there to wherever you desire or become the sky
And then like rain come plummeting back to earth.
What not you can do, what not you can achieve?

Om, Om, Om, it is only Om, Om, Om.

Walk with Krishna to sprint with infinity towards eternity,
Dip in the ocean of God and come out sparklingly clean.
Weave dreams into reality and in reality, become real.
Make now eternal and in that moment of nowness become immortal;
Caress impossibilities with the possibility of a Krishna wand,
With one stride go beyond where even beyond is captivated.
Om, Om, Om, it is only Om, Om, Om.

The power you have you can never guess, nor think,
What you can imagine you can never imagine, so think,
Conquering demons is nothing, conquer Godliness, just think,
With Krishna what elevation you can get, for a second, think,
You can attract the gopis of goodness with Krishna's flute, think,
In your own world, the entire universe can fit, so a while, think.
Om, Om, Om, it is only Om, Om, Om.

Be ignorant of all, be aware of Krishna only, that is awakening;
When you awaken you never need to sleep nor rest nor be active.
Into statelessness you pass, where there's nothing, no one, nobody,

Oneness is all that is, only Oneness, and in that Oneness, you are one.

Change venom into nectar, depression into joy, emptiness into fulfilment,

Hold Krishna's finger and become the hand of god, attain eternal glory.

Om, Om, Om, it is only Om, Om, Om.

21. Bond With Banke

Become the link between Time and Timelessness
And be timeless in Time, so don't fret over time;
Blake held eternity in an hour, you can, in a moment,
Krishna is Time, but Time is not Krishna, nothing can be, he,
Ride the vehicle of misery or become a medium of joy.
Short-lived joys are aplenty, that doesn't serve the purpose,
A purposeless life takes you away from your cosmic goal.
Don't look for motive, be the motive, the reason for delight,
Wipe a tear, offer a smile, give alleviation in exchange of pain.
Bond with Banke, blend with Banwari, be blessed by Brijmohan.

Towards a mandatory end the world is moving, move first,
With Krishna get a head start so that you never look behind;
Lead the way, be your own leader, rest leave it on Pyare, pyare,
Amidst mud find diamond, in desert discover greenery, search,
See what you obtain when you say Om only once, say it to experience.

Dance with Damodar and gods will see you perform on cosmic stage;

Become centre stage, the centre point, the core, the essence of self.
The line to reach God is endless, become the bridge that takes
Every devotee to Him so that Krishna sends your stock soaring,
To reach the pinnacle of piety bow as much as possible to Parthasarathy.

Wildernesses turn into evergreen forests, puddles become oceans,
Black coal sparkles like a minor sun, night appears like dewy morn,
Distance between earth and sky disappears, hut becomes heaven,
What you want you don't want for you get more than you can think;
Miracles happen when you sing Om Hari Om, Om Hari Om.

Om, the precious sound, Om, the valuable sound, Om, the sound,
Om gives meaning to meaninglessness, without Om, all is zilch,
Om soothes, placates, elevates, stirs, takes you to other worlds,
The starting sound, the prehistoric sound, the sound of life and living,
The universal sound, the universe sound, the godly sound.

Life can be lifeless, lifeless can become life, it's all about attitude;
There are certain ways, fixed trails, but you can carve your own paths,
Be a pathbreaker, a trailblazer, recite Om one hundred eight times,

Open your *sahasrara* and become attuned with the other chakras,
With Om rise and rise and rise and rise and rise and rise and rise.
Keep transforming, there's newness in every moment, bask in it.
Revel in the vibration of Om, surrender to its charm, resist not,
For resistance to Om is not possible, willingly, unwillingly one has to give in;
So, surrender willingly to its power and divineness, become its spokesperson,
Om, Om, Om, slowly, gently, lyrically, rhythmically, Om, Om, Om.
All the way, at every step, awake, asleep, aware, what drives you is Om,
Be driven by Om, be spurred by Om, be motivated by Om; say Om, Om,
Within, without, wherever, whatever, whenever, Om, Om, Om, Om, Om,

Deliver with Om, decide with Om, decipher with Om, declare with Om,
From womb until tomb the only sound worth hearing and speaking is Om.

22. From Zero To Zillion

Brahma, Vishnu, Shiva, curve, crescent, dot, wake, dream, sleep,
Oceanic waves, cosmic pull, soul's magnetism, mind's opening,

This world, that world, world in world, all worlds, all universes,
Connect, disconnect, attach, detach, merge, demerge, zero, infinity,
The grind, the pastime, the blue in the blue sky, the green in the leaves.

Immutable, incalculable, indomitable, inexhaustible, imperishable,
The colours in the rainbow, the vastness in vast, the eternal circle,
Peace, tranquility, unity, yoga, health, wealth, wisdom, spirituality.

While on the move, while in a trance, while idle, while stateless,
For Zen in life, for zest in life, for zeal in life, from zero to zillion,

For that spark, for that spur, for that spunk, for that sensation.

Conscience, chaste conscience, consciousness, super consciousness,
The unravelling of mysteries, the decoding of secrets, the clear way,
The unknotting of the mind, the liberation of the soul, delightful sway,
The sacred formula, the mysterious mantra, the meaningful music.

Earth, atmosphere, heaven, thought, speech, action, the Vedas,
Goodness, passion, darkness, all that is from the beginning, all before,
Where mind is boggled, where thought is bamboozled,
Where there is no where, where there is no there, where, there, nothing.

Make monotony mesmerizing, make ordinary extraordinary, excel,
Blow away the blowing winds of pain, whistle away your agonies.

The power of Om is such you will become powerful from within;

Your soul will sing songs of spirituality and your mind of mysticism,
Moments of bliss will surround you and you will surround Time.

Into nothingness will fade your inner self and you'll be free of *moksha*,
Sweetly, hypnotically, Om will affect you and free you from all addictions;
Addiction of desires, addiction of wealth, addiction of world.

If you are drawn to the Infinite, Infinite is drawn to you,
Understand the potential inside you, bring it outside you, at once,
Conquering the world is nothing, conquering the self is everything.

Standing atop the mountain is an achievement of courage and bravery;
The mountain standing on your little finger is a thing of divinity.

Shut your mind to the noises around you, open it to only one sound, Om,
Let this sound enter every pore of your body, let every pore vibrate with it.

Become your own Brahma, your own Vishnu, your own Shiva,
Create newer you, administer present you, destroy the bad you, be your god.

Self-belief comes with Om, and so does confidence, and so also godly poise;
Om, Om, Om, from head to toe, from earth to heaven, from this to that,
That's the word that empowers you to convert uncertainty into a leap of faith.

One step is enough to master yourself, take that one step, say Om,
The mind is a devil when it comes to godly matters, so beware, say Om.

23. Om Echoes In Every Echo

Om breaks through all barriers;
Those who chant become warriors.
Make it a daily habit, recite all day,
Every chant will open a new way.

Earth and heaven and life and death;
Your mind, body and every breath,
Om is omnipresent, Om is omniscient,
For self-realisation, it is sufficient.

Make demons your best of best friends,
With its chant reach goals, change trends,
Look at everything with a newer angle,
It will make your heart and soul jangle.

Worlds of dreams get created within you,
For others you become a perfect view.
You can tower above the clear blue sky
And shine like the sun that shines so high.

There are no limits to what you can achieve;
Miraculous gifts from heaven you'll receive.

Your soul will become radiantly brilliant,
Your spirit will become tough and resilient.

Discover a new you then enhance the new;
Be the grass, the sky, the cloud, and the dew.
From every pore of your body let Om emanate
Within and without you, let Om resonate.

Listen to the pebble singing at the wayside,
Hear the oceanic sound when it's high n low tide,
Inspire inspiration, motivate motivation, say Om,
This sound is in bubble and froth, sizzle and foam.

Riding on Om gallop away into the cosmos,
Imprint yourself on the sky, front, back, across.
Add glow to light, clean to purity, virtue to devotion,
Enhance your inner self with plenty of Om emotion.

Om echoes in every echo, be it earth or space,
In all the sounds, the sound of Om one can trace;
All tunes, low and high, all pitches, high and low,
In a bird's melody, in a leaf's flutter, in Time's flow.

Om is a rhythm, a musical ecstasy, a lyrical delight,
When you go deep into Om, your soul takes flight.
Make the most of the moment, make it boundless,

The sound of Om emerges from even the soundless.

Om rules the world of mysticism; gives mystics power,
From the bud of disbelief, Om makes faith, flower,
Let not anything pester you, or anyone disturb you,
What wonders Om can work for you, you've no clue.

Sun, moon, stars, are the toys that will surround,
The cosmic world will be like your playground.
Om, Om, Om, go on chanting this ultimate mantra,
Become the author of life, practice your own tantra.

With the colour of rainbow paint your mindscape;
Into newer worlds every day you can escape.
The limitless will shrink and you will expand,
Even the ant to you will appear grand.

Om connects you to the ultimate connection,
It removes from your life all distraction.
When you submerge yourself in the sound of Om,
You rise to heavenly heights and in heavens you roam.

Add hope to the song of hope, make it more hopeful;
Join the fragments of peace and make it peaceful.
From the shades of uncertainty, create conviction,
Turn into realities your life's every lie and fiction.
Om can take you on a ride of a lifetime, so be ready,

Despite your inconsistencies, it makes your feet steady.
Om will convert all your failings into a sea of success,
Great powers, Om will make you possess.

Swim in life's ocean, splash in the pool of eternity;
In God's vast kingdom, build your own big city.
Live on until you wish, die only when you desire,
Chanting of Om makes you go higher and higher.

Om is in the hush of silence, in the boom of volcano,
Om unravels mysteries, opens secrets, so that you know.
The door of knowledge is always ready to welcomes you,
All that is old and ancient turns for you modern and new.

Pierce the core of darkness, welcome the golden dawn,
Transform a thorny trail into a well-manicured lawn.
Unleash your potential, become the throb of the universe,
Write odes to life and love, and for Krishna pen a verse.

Extol the virtues of the blue-god, praise him to the hilt,
With every word of praise, make him towards you, tilt.
His mere glance will change the wheels of your fate,
You'll turn from bad to good and from good to great.

Shri Krishna Govinda Hare Murari will sweeten life,
Your existence will be free from struggles and strife.
Om Sri Krishna sharanam namah will give you shelter,

The discord between mind and heart will run helter-skelter.

You are the trophy, you are the game, you are the player,
Let only Krishna judge you, he is the god, he is the prayer.
He is the one who bridges the gap between Self and Light;
He is the one who stands between wrong and right.

Tame the wild in you, make wild the tame in you, do whatever;
Live life like a god and make death, life too, thus live forever.
At your beck and call the universe can be, do Krishna's bidding;
All ills, harms and evils that hang around you will go skidding.

Become the cause for all great causes, embrace immortality;
Overwhelm meanness around you with Krishna's generosity.
Om's force will sweep you away to a country of nirvana,
Where you won't be distracted by any devil or madonna.

Fix bulbs of halo, chandeliers of aura, illumine your soul,
Split into fragments and in the debris see yourself as whole.
For the sightless become the vision, seek horizons new,
Show intensity to meet Krishna and you can skip the queue.

Keep whispering Om, Om, Om, all the while, all the time,
Your soul will become beautiful and your mind sublime.
Change the scenes of your life, the landscapes of your dreams,

Write the script of your choice, choose your own themes.

The life you lead can become the life God wants you to lead;
With Krishna in mind, Om on lips, nothing more you'd need.
The sky for you can become the beginning of your elevation;
Learn Krishna, for from head to toe he is steeped in education.

Dig into yourself, go deeper if required, you will find him,
The light that Krishna ignites in you will never grow dim.
Walk like a king; if you are Krishna's, the world is yours,
This life, death, and your rebirths, for you he firmly secures.

To sweeten your life, drink the venom of penance, sacrifice,
Every hellish situation for you Krishna will turn into paradise.
When you say Om very often, you become as chaste as Sita,
Your breaths will be like the holy shlokas of Bhagavad Gita.

In unreal conditions be real, and be like Buddha in the real state,
With Krishna's blessings become the captain of your fate.
When you idolize Krishna, your image gets glorified manifold
And on every nuance of life, you acquire a stranglehold.

In the Order of Things, you'll catapult to the foremost place,
Amongst the pious and the holy you'll have the strongest case.

With the successful in heaven, you'll hold the banner of victory,
Embrace Lord Krishna and from all the worries become free.

Turn all anguish into eternal joy and all joy into eternal peace;
Become so contented that all desires, your soul will release.
From the wilderness of obscurity emerge in the oasis of prominence,
Say Om Krishna Om Krishna to get over yourself total dominance.

24. The Endless Flight

Away, away, the sound of Om takes you.

Like a tireless bird flying over mountains and oceans,
You too fly on and on.

The endless flight.

Where every scene is out of God's private collection;
Where bliss is not a destination, but the beginning of a journey.

The endless flight.

The sun is your companion, you play with him;
With stars you sleep in the heavenly bed.

The endless flight.

Away, away, the sound of Om takes you.

25. Drown In The Sound Of Om

Amidst the chaos of the world, find your own island.

Om, Om, Om, drown in this sound, Om, Om, Om.

Ascend above your imagination, redefine every thought.

Om, Om, Om, drown in this sound, Om, Om, Om.

The depths of your soul deepen, a spring of wellness gushes.

Om, Om, Om, drown in this sound, Om, Om, Om.

Live a dreamlike life, make every moment memorable.

Om, Om, Om, drown in this sound, Om, Om, Om.

Be God's ally, become a force to be reckoned with.

Om, Om, Om, drown in this sound, Om, Om, Om.

26. Glory Be To The Chanters Of Om

Glory be to the chanters of Om;
May their tribe build castles in heaven!

The river of hope flows relentlessly,
The sacred rain falls incessantly.

In the parched land of desires,
A garden of fulfilment flowers majestically.

The soul sings merrily an ancient song,
That song heals the wounds of the present.

From the cages of doubt, birds of freedom
Sneak out into the open air and fly to a land of certainty.

Glory be to the chanters of Om;
May their tribe build castles in heaven!

27. Om, Om, Om

The unmaking of man, the making of God,
In Krishna's eyes, only love is for you.
That what you can't see, that what you can't do,
Set sight on him and transform your destiny.

Echoes of love reverberate inside the soul;
Fallen angels rise like a phoenix from the ashes,
A dead-end is neither dead nor an end;
Life starts with a cry.

Om, Om, Om.

Inside the innermost self is a mirror;
That mirror reflects harmony.
When thoughts turn into pandemonium,
Look in that mirror.

An hour of nap with complete faith,
A night spent worshipping in doubt,
The contrast is so appalling,
Life becomes so challenging.

Om, Om, Om.

28. A Krishna-Filled Soul

Motionless Time and Time in motion;
A Krishna-filled soul, the game changer,
The destruction of thought and notion;
In the forest of life, you are the lone ranger.

Carve out dreams from nightmarish states;
Restore the ruins, be a painter of delight.
Inspire the world of others and their fates,
Create many nirvanas during day and night.

Stand atop any mountain of your choice,
But first capture the Everest of ego in you.
Make the mind your friend, then rejoice,
Every moment you'll be a person new.

Om catapults you to spheres beyond spheres;
Meet the Universe Boss eye to eye, be firm,
In a flash, in any form, and anywhere, he appears,
Be kind even to the squirming, squiggling worm.

Travel through eras, become a part of Time,
Merge with Krishna, conquer the soul.
Be the reason, the song, the purpose, the rhyme,

In every way, of life, be in total control.

29. Om Namah Shivay

The vibration that vibrates the self,
It stirs immortality within the mortals.
Intense darkness becomes a sea of light,
The soul leaps over the boundless universe.

Turn the Casanova in you into a monk;
Like a nomad traverse the paths of heaven,
When nothingness also matters not to you,
Then something in you catches a spark.

Sweeten every bitterness, brighten the dimness,
Make sorrow laugh, bring smile on dullness,
Seize the moment, capture the glory,
Fulfill the fulfilment, surrender to the sound.

Om Namah Shivay.

30. Om Gam Ganapataye Namaha

O Lord of Beginnings
Make our beginnings successful;

Remove the hurdles in our way,
Make us sprint in the race of life.

Shower your blessings, O Deva,
Make us bathe in your generosity.

Convert every thorn in our path
Into an aromatic flower,
Tend the gardens of our soul;

Awaken our conscience, let us rise,
Give us the gift to make our spirits prosper.

Om Gam Ganapataye Namaha.

31. Om Mani Padme Hum

Unknown, we are, make us known, O Known,
What we know is that we know nothing we know,
O Known give us knowledge, give us wisdom.

Cold we are to situations around us, thaw us,
With your warmth ignite in us, feelings,
O the Compassionate, make us compassionate.

Impatiently, we grab at fleeting moments, but miss,
The colossus Time passes us by, we die every moment;
O the Most Patient One, make Time still for us.

We become enraged over your own creations
For matters trifle and at times without reason,
Give us a balanced mind, O Lord of Equanimity.

Where there's grief, let there be limitless joy,
Where there's joy, let there be a nirvanic pause,
In that nirvanic pause, let our lives throb.

Om Mani Padme Hum.

32. Om Aeem Bhreem Hanumate

The impediments are many and we are worried;
The end is closing in on us, we are in a fix.
Swallow the sun of sorrow on our behalf,
For you, it's just like eating a fruit,
O Sankat – Mochan, come to our aid, make us happy.

Make us human, O Super-God, hone us, chisel us,
The way you expanded and shrunk yourself
When Surasa threatened you with her size,
O Pavanputra help us to leap beyond impossibilities
Into the kingdom of possibilities;

Om Aeem Bhreem Hanumate
Shree Ram Dootaaya Namaha.

33. Hare Krishna

Dance with the moonbeams, make the darkness yours,
In the abyss of ignorance, light a candle of enlightenment.
Step into a whole new world, merge with infinity,
Dwarf greatness with your achievements, pierce the cosmos,
Leave your stamp on the atmosphere.

Find yourself in yourself before attempting to find the One,
Connect the dots of doubt that are scattered within you.
March across the dry landscape of your withered mind,
Water it with the knowledge of Krishna, beckon him,
Imprint your soul with his image.

Embody Truth in every action, act like a true Krishna *bhakt*,
Sever ties with falsehood, forever become clean, clear, certain.
Shake hands with God, shake off all your inhibitions,
Build a monument of splendour, become splendid in what you do,
Carve a niche in Krishna's heart.

Hare Krishna, Hare Krishna, Krishna, Krishna.

34. Om Shanti Om

The ocean of time flows,
The face of the universe glows.
Om makes silence, silent;
Brings peace to the violent.

Breathe in, breathe out,
Be quiet or when you shout,
Om is in the air all the time;
In speech, silence and in mime.

The path to glory is through Om;
Let Om in your body always roam.
Om was when the world was not,
Om will be when the world will be naught.

Om Shanti Om, Om Shanti Om,
Recite this miraculous psalm.
For the well-being of the soul
And to become a part of the Whole.

35. Beyond Every Beyond

An effulgent soul reverberates with Om echoes;
Darkness vanishes as if it never existed.
Beyond every beyond, this sound persists,
The rainbow-filled sky bends to kiss your lips.

Every anguish transforms into bliss;
The dynamics of life swing in your favour.
Within a flash, lights brilliantly shine,
From being in limelight, you become the limelight.

The mind darts from earth to cosmos,
Then from cosmos to boundaries unknown.
Your ascension is endless, you keep elevating,
Every dimension gets conquered.

You become a secret beyond anyone's understanding;
In the company of gods, you create your own space.
Om gains God's goodwill for you, you become so special,
Transcending Life and Death, you float away to immortality.

36. Become A Landmark For Others

Penetrate life's deepest soul, pierce the core of happiness,
Become the ruler of the land of attainment, rule forever,
Pluck stars from the sky like you'd fruits from a tree,
Stir energy in places where there's none possible.

Turn obscurity into fame, dark into dazzle, nothing into everything,
Sculpt hopelessness into hope, helplessness into power, create synergy.
Between now and next and before and after and moments and memories
Establish your own set of rules, fix the misery, revel in sheer bliss.

Build glory into glorious, knock down need into needless,
Give birth to inspirations, develop idleness into ideas.
Play with fate, make fear, fearless, triumph over every adversity,
Synchronize with Om to make disagreements, harmonious.

Shimmer in darkness, in a desert be an oasis, over parched land fall like rain,

In scarcity be abundance, in heat be shade, in winter warmth,
Be the glue that binds heart, be the spirit that boosts spirits,
be in aloneness,
Become a landmark for others in their journey of spirituality.

37. From Dusks Create Dawns

Penetrate life's deepest soul, pierce the core of happiness,
Become the ruler of the land of attainment, rule forever,
Pluck stars from the sky like you'd fruits from a tree,
Stir energy in places where there's none possible.

Turn obscurity into fame, dark into dazzle, nothing into everything,
Sculpt hopelessness into hope, helplessness into power, create synergy.
Between now and next and before and after and moments and memories
Establish your own set of rules, fix the misery, revel in sheer bliss.

Build glory into glorious, knock down need into needless,
Give birth to inspirations, develop idleness into ideas.
Play with fate, make fear, fearless, triumph over every adversity,
Synchronize with Om to make disagreements, harmonious.

Shimmer in darkness, in a desert be an oasis, over parched land fall like rain,

In scarcity be abundance, in heat be shade, in winter warmth,
Be the glue that binds heart, be the spirit that boosts spirits,
be in aloneness,
Become a landmark for others in their journey of spirituality.

38. Om

Om
The melody of the universe,
The song of the soul,
The tune of enlightenment,
The lyric of the mind,
The poetry of Gods.

Om
The sound that enchants,
The echo that educates,
The hum of harmony,
The resonance of spirituality,
The reverberation of intellect.

Om
The heart's throb,
The tongue's rhythm,
The voice of conscience,
The mother of language,
The sound of sounds.

Om
The chant of eternity,

The hymn of infinity,
The carol of perpetuity,
The chorus of angels,
The celebration of divinity.

Om
From heaven to earth,
From one end to another,
From beginning to end,
From then to now,
From here to beyond.

Om
Makes vacuum vibrate,
Fills emptiness,
Creates nirvanic milestones,
Removes hindrances,
Eliminates negativity.

Om
The immortal sound,
The eternal call,
The limitless energy,
The vital in vitality,
The potency in strength.

Om

The charm,
The talisman,
The magnet,
The ornament,
The magic.

Om
The rattle that rattles the rivals,
The tone that sets the tone for tranquility,
The jingle that justifies justice,
The chime that creates creativity,
The rhyme of reasoning and rationalisation.

Om
Brahma's boom,
Vishnu's verse,
Shiva's sonnet,
Ganesh's gurgle,
Ram's rhapsody.

Om
The peak of ecstasy,
The acme of delight,
The pinnacle of nirvana,
The height of spirituality,
The apex of self-realisation.

Om
Spurs you to achieve goals,
Converts impossibilities into possibilities,
Gives you a fillip to rise,
Enhances your inner set-up,
Rejuvenates your spiritual being.
Om
The vibe of positivity,
The connect with divinity,
The emotion of piety,
The soul of sanctity,
The heart of devotion.

Om
Demolishes doubt,
Builds faith,
Strengthens belief,
Creates newer you,
Unravels mysteries.

Om
Brings you closer to God,
Opens the door of secrets,
Takes you on a heavenly flight,
Submerges you in the pool of mysticism,
Elevates you to unheard of loftiness.

Om
Transcends,
Translates,
Transmutes,
Transforms,
Transmits.

Om
A way of life,
The garden of bliss,
A mind of its own,
The inspiration,
A heaven in heaven.

About The Author

Author- Nasir Zaidi

Nasir Zaidi is an ex-banker, stock-market investor, portfolio advisor, blogger, gourmet, hodophile and cricket enthusiast.

Born in Kajgaon in the district of Jaunpur in Uttar Pradesh, he was educated at Rose Manor Garden School and Sacred Heart Boy's High School in Mumbai. His life took a somersault when in a biology practical class, he had to dissect a frog. Unable to do that, he left the laboratory. For some days, he pondered over life and its mysteries. And then, one fine day, he left for the Himalayan Kingdom, where he spent his time reading, meditating and studying Buddhism. After his homecoming, he obtained a Master's degree in English literature from Bombay University and then a PGD (Postgraduate Diploma) in journalism.

His aim in life was to become a vagabond cum writer. But his mother made him a banker. She persuaded him to sit for Bombay Mercantile Cooperative (BMC) Bank's exam, which he successfully cleared. From BMC Bank, he moved to Development Credit Bank (DCB) and then to Commercial Bank of Dubai (CBD). In between all this, in the early 2000s, he taught creative writing at Somaiya Institute.

After spending over twenty-five years in the banking sector in various capacities, he decided to finally listen to his heart. In August 2021, he published his first book, *My Own Heaven in God's Kingdom*, a collection of poems on Imam Ali. *Om: The Timeless Sound* is his second book. He is now writing a novel.

He is married to Farhat, a student success coach by profession, with whom he has two children – a son, Saamish, and a daughter, Insia. He can be contacted on his personal email ID: nasirzaidi27@yahoo.com.

www.ingramcontent.com/pod-product-compliance
Ingram Content Group UK Ltd.
Pitfield, Milton Keynes, MK11 3LW, UK
UKHW040009200726
13854UKWH00001B/114

9 798885 467346